Visions of Alba

Scenes from Scotland's History

Visions of Alba

Scenes from Scotland's History

Thor Ewing

WELKIN BOOKS

First Published 2015
Welkin Books Ltd

Poem II was originally published in Simply Scottish Magazine, 2012.

ISBN 978-1-910075-02-9

Contents

Columba was exiled from Ireland for his role in the Battle of Cúl Dreimhne, which was fought over his copy of St Finnian's psalm book. In atonement he came to Scotland as a missionary, where he was granted land on Iona in 563. After his death in 597, his bones remained on the island until 849, when they were removed for safety. His relics were enshrined in the Brecbennoch and, in 1314 they were present at the Battle of Bannockburn.

I

Iona AD597

A book brought me—a book and a battle.
That battle became my life, and I
the champion of the King of Kings.
My shaven-haired warriors practice each day
at prayer in the cloister—their weapons
the psalms which they sing from my book.

When my Lord gathers me up, they will
lay out my bones on this blessed isle.

The Pictish king, Angus II, led his army to victory over the Angles at Athelstaneford in the name of St Andrew. According to medieval chroniclers, this victory was marked by the sign of St Andrew's Saltire in the clouds overhead, and the symbol was taken up in the Scottish flag.

II

Athelstaneford AD832

The blue sky smiles down on the field,
where the fallen cry out with their wounds.
Not Angus but Andrew has led us this day;
it is he who brought us victory. Our enemy
fled before us to Berwick and beyond.

Blessed be Andrew the Martyr!
White clouds unfurl his cross, outspread
through the heavens above Athelstaneford.

King Alexander III was the last king of the House of Dunkeld, descended from the semi-legendary Fergus Mór, King of Dál Riata, who died in 501. When Alexander was killed in a riding accident at Pettycur in 1286, the regular path of hereditary kingship in Scotland was broken for ever.

III

North Queensferry
18 March 1286

The treacherous passage over the Forth
now accomplished, hoofs strike
hard on the unmetalled road
as the king's horse surges forwards.

He'll ride on now without a guide—the gathering dark
can hold no fears for the heart that hopes to
greet a tender sweetheart, and his horse's feet
know well the road from here by Pettycur.

Perhaps the most famous blow in Scottish history is Robert Bruce's killing of the young English knight Henry de Bohun. Bruce had been addressing the troops before the battle, when de Bohun saw the unarmoured king and charged. Because of his contested hereditary claim to the Crown, Scots recognised King Robert "inasmuch as he saved our people, and for upholding our freedom" (Declaration of Arbroath, 1320).

IV

Bannockburn
23 June 1314

A shout from the ranks. The king
brings his palfrey round to face the horseman
thundering forwards, sunlight dancing
on burnished armour. Hold still.

A hundred yards—his fingers close
around his axe as the knight lowers his lance.
Fifty yards—his spurs touch the horse's sides as,
axe aloft, he ducks around the lance-head for the kill.

We know enough of Queen Mary Stewart's opinions and upbringing to guess something of her feelings on taking up the Scottish monarchy. Her fond adieu to France is well-known, and the French opinion of Scottish attitudes to social class is also a matter of record. This poem imagines her private inner monologue on the evening of her triumphal arrival in Edinburgh.

V

The Queen's Chambers, Holyrood
19 August 1561

Scotland! Rude in its countryside, in its
mountains and its moorlands; rude in its
cooking, stewed meats with oats and barley;
rude in its arts and in its music; where
the greatest lord shakes hands with
the meanest peasant and calls him kin.

O France! Did I forsake my dearest home
for the rule of this unruly kingdom?

When the English queen Elizabeth I died in the early hours of 24 March 1603, Robert Carey, Earl of Monmouth, set out for Edinburgh to tell King James VI that he had inherited the throne of England, Wales, Ireland and the Channel Islands. After three days hard riding, stopping only to change horses, he reached the king in his bedchamber at midnight. Although Monmouth's errand earned him the scorn of the English gentry, James rewarded him with the post of Governor to the future King Charles I.

VI

The Forecourt, Holyrood
26 March 1603

The night air rings with hoofbeats on the cobbles.
Inside, the King of Scots lies sleeping.
With weary urgency, a rider
swings down from his saddle.

His foot does not yet touch the ground;
the palace doors are not yet open.
The news, which for three hard days has driven
this nobleman north from London, has yet to be told.

Flora McCambridge and the baby Ranald MacDonald of Sanda were among a very few survivors of the Siege of Dunaverty, which began on 31 May 1647. According to tradition, Flora was able to escape because she and the baby were wearing a tartan associated with the Campbells and their allies rather than with the MacDonalds. Although the elaborate system of clan tartans known today is the creation of the Clan Revival, some form of recognition by tartan seems to have been possible even in the seventeenth and eighteenth centuries.

The Great Feud between Campbells and MacDonalds saw few acts of mercy on either side, but it has been claimed that Flora's tartan plaid was the gift of an anonymous Campbell clansman. It should also be noted that the attackers were not exclusively Campbells, but included Covenanters of Highland and Lowland names.

VII

Dunaverty Castle
early June 1647

They spared not age nor innocence,
not childhood nor womanhood. And I,
with the wide-eyed wean at my breast
was ready to meet their cruel dirks, until
this youth, this blessed lad wrapped
his piece of patterned plaid around us.

That tartan was the pass, which let a daughter of
MacDonald walk free between the Campbell blades.

In 1679, a Covenanter conventicle gathered near Loudoun Hill to hear the preaching of Rev. Thomas Douglas. When they learned that the dragoons of John Graham of Claverhouse were coming against them, 200 Covenanters took up a position behind boggy ground at Drumclog. After an exchange of fire, the Covenanters attacked and routed the Royalist dragoons.
The Covenant of 1638 revived the National Covenant of 1581 to which King James VI was a party, and which was theoretically binding on his heirs.

VIII

High Drumclog
1 June 1679

We gathered not for battle but to worship
our Lord, according to the Covenant that is
between us, our God and our king—
there never was room therein for a bishop!

It is not we who have broken faith.
If the king is against us, we have
God on our side. Let the Lord
destroy the army of Pharaoh!

At the Battle of Killiecrankie, Williamite forces under General Hugh Mackay of Scourie were attacked and routed in a matter of minutes by Jacobites under the command of John Graham of Claverhouse. Two thousand government troops were killed, but one Donald MacBean made good his escape at a spot still known as The Soldier's Leap. Claverhouse was killed in the moment of his victory, and his cause would soon be defeated at the Battle of Dunkeld.

IX

Killiecrankie
27 July 1689

Minutes ago he was marching forwards, in
uniform, in line and in order, following the flag
and the throbbing drum, deeper into the wooded valley.

Now he is running blindly, helter-skelter through
the undergrowth—running back, running
anywhere, running away from the shouted
slogans and the cries of his dying comrades.
At the cliff's edge, he leaps.

1st and 2nd Companies, The Earl of Argyll's Regiment of Foot were billeted with the MacIains of Glencoe to collect the Cess Tax, when they received the order to "fall upon the rebels [and] put all to the sword." Thirty eight clansmen were killed and forty women and children died of exposure in the aftermath. The death toll could easily have been far higher, but this unpopular order was rather ineffectually carried out. Lieut. Francis Farquhar and Lieut. Gilbert Kennedy each broke his own sword rather than take part in the massacre. Although they were initially arrested, the two lieutenants were fully exonerated and later gave evidence against their commanding officers.

X

Glencoe
12 February 1692

Let them shoot me for it! This sword
has been my badge of honour since
first I enlisted to fight for King William
and the love of my God. How can
we serve our God, when we betray
our hosts for the sake of our king?

I cannot break the bonds of justice,
so now I have broken my sword.

Anne, Duchess of Hamilton, was the first signatory to the Edinburgh book of the Darien Scheme, which aimed to rival English merchant endeavours with a trading company and colony on the isthmus of Panama. The result was disastrous. Coming hard on the heels of a run of 'ill years' in which Scotland had suffered a series of poor harvests, the massive financial losses suffered by Scotland's ruling elite left the country facing ruin.

XI

Hamilton Palace
circa 1700

Three thousand pounds of my own,
and thousands more from across the kingdom!
How many thousands of lives
of our poor Scots men?

Our king and John Company have scuppered the nation!
The ship of Scotland foundered on the reef of false promise!
This barren adventure has wrecked all our hopes!
How I wish I had never heard of Darien.

Parliament debated the proposed political union with England at length. This poem draws on speeches by William Seton of Pitmedden and John Hamilton, Lord Bellhaven, which seem to sum up the opposing arguments. Seton's view is one of sober resignation, while Bellhaven's expresses the tragedy incurred when any independent nation is compelled to surrender sovereignty.

XII

Parliament House, Edinburgh 15th November 1706

A king with two kingdoms must ever
prefer the stronger over the weaker. It is
Union with England or with France, and
in France lies certain war with England.

Yet do you see how our Mother Caledonia
sits among us, stripped naked but for
the flag she clutches to her breast, while we
clamour to raise our dirks against her?

www.ingramcontent.com/pod-product-compliance
Ingram Content Group UK Ltd.
Pitfield, Milton Keynes, MK11 3LW, UK
UKHW041950190726
13854UKWH00004B/1879